ALL CLEAR

Publication of this book was supported by a grant from
the Eric Mathieu King Fund of The Academy of American Poets.

THE
James
DICKEY
CONTEMPORARY POETRY SERIES

EDITED BY RICHARD HOWARD

ALL CLEAR

Poems by Robert Hahn

UNIVERSITY OF SOUTH CAROLINA PRESS

Published in Columbia, South Carolina, by the
University of South Carolina Press 5/3/97

Manufactured in the United States of America

00 99 98 97 96   5 4 3 2 1

Library of Congress Cataloging-in-Publication Data

Hahn, Robert, 1938–
    All Clear : poems / by Robert Hahn
        p.   cm. — (The James Dickey contemporary poetry series)
        ISBN 1–57003–132–0 (cloth) . — ISBN 1–57003–133–9 (paper)
        I. Title. II. Series.
    PS3558.A3236A79   1996
    811' .54 —dc20   96–4461

For Nicole Rafter

Light of my life,
Partner in crime.

CONTENTS

PART III

A NOTE ON ROBERT HAHN

Anything but a raw recruit to his art, indeed more likely to strike the reader as a practiced, though hardly hardened, veteran (his adept and much-exercised voice has not been heard, been *scored,* for some while: almost a decade since the last chapbook), Robert Hahn is a poet of what Emerson calls "beyonding"—it is necessary for him to ground his perceptions, his discoveries in a specific circumstance, to write around the occasion, *to circumscribe* in order to ascend. As he says so powerfully in "False Dawn":

> . . . How one loves the impassioned drudgery
> of names, decoding a bunker, a mosque enjambed
> with Venetian stone, the world demystified.

(As for veteran expertise, I rest my case with the axiological force of *enjambed* here, a truly beguiled usage.)

Throughout Hahn's knowledgeable book such "impassioned drudgery" will be strenuously indulged (though for us, of course, it is no such thing: naming is glamour, glossy as well as glossary, on the receiving end) in order to reach the risen condition, the *state beyond* which is the purpose of all his poems. I cite the poet once again in order to assert the Understood Relation (which will bring forth the secretest man of blood, as Macbeth calls it):

> Simple men, we like to assume,
> Obedient to the blunt instructions of [our] master: be
> composed. Tell the truth.

As often as not, such orders come from the painters and novelists, who are faithfully studied here as docents of levitation. How studious, indeed how worldly Robert Hahn appears in his inspection of the nostalgias, the makings, the shrines. Not much escapes the punctual cunning of his notation as he observes what Wordsworth called "fallings from us, vanishings."

. . . The acknowledgment of imperfections, of veritable collapse, the abasement of culture seems to be necessary, or at least concomitant, if we are to soar to any height; it is a measure of Hahn's passionate elevation in almost every one of his grand poems that the scrubbed missions, the underminings, the duds, are so inveterately accounted for, ruefully, gingerly, but with all the sharpness of some other ripened spice, a secret ingredient.

It is a great privilege to partisan the poetry of a master—but I want to clarify the kind of mastery involved here (and *involved* is surely the right word, the sense expressed of being at the heart of the matter, in deep): not so much the delighted control of the medium, the eager display of the wonderful articulations, though these are the first matters to come to light, as the mastery of what we call "experience," the mystery of a world revealed when the conditions for apprehension are, yes indeed, *all clear.*

Richard Howard

ACKNOWLEDGMENTS

Grateful acknowledgment is made to these publications in which the following poems first appeared:

The Antioch Review:
>   Wittgenstein Eats

Carolina Quarterly:
>   April in L.A.
>   One More Time

The Centennial Review:
>   Attending (as "The Rainbow Over Lake Buttermere")
>   Five Views of This and the Other World

The Denver Quarterly:
>   Shelburne Farms Coachyard, Swallows, Schubert

The Iowa Review:
>   Desperado
>   Interior at Petworth

The New Republic:
>   Martinis, Maidens, Midnight Hours

The Paris Review:
>   All Clear
>   Conversation With a Dealer
>   "MOB RULES"
>   Olmsted's Fens Corrected by Shircliff
>   Summer and Winter at the Mount
>   Tell the Truth

Southwest Review:
>   Sundown at Santa Cruz

The Western Humanities Review:
> Angels
> Copying
> Memories of Texas Falls
> Venice Obscured

The following poems, some in earlier versions and under different titles, appeared in One More Time, *The Cummington Press, 1988.*

April in L.A.; Desperado; Interior at Petworth; One More Time; Out of the Blue; Photograph; Shelburne Farms Coachyard, Swallows, Schubert; Wittgenstein Eats.

ALL CLEAR

PART I

ALL CLEAR

Drums. Cannon. Punishing rain. Lightning
    Has roused the auto-theft alarms
On Avenue Beaumarchais to an eerie siren-
    Wail of grief, or something like it—

What's the trouble? Out on my balcony I see:
    The sidewalk streaming with verdigris
And rosso in gleaming black, and cars chased
    As they turn the corner by alter egos,

And new faces blooming: in a martial quick-step
    The balcony *en face* fills with a crew-cut
And khaki t-shirt. Hmph! Nothing requires
    His attention. He bangs his shutters

While over his head a woman in a red dress
    Is flinging open drawers and cabinets,
Almost dancing—expecting a lover? Or stunned
    By the never- or always-expected message,

All is lost! Cornell's boxes empty
    And fill . . . doesn't he remind you, the guy
Scratching his head, in the rumpled white pajamas,
    Of a silent comedy hero sweetly

Bemused (Harry Langdon?) as chaos swirls
    Around him. . . . Tugging his sleeve, the girl-
Friend is the ingenue, kittenish but matter-of-fact:
    Back to bed! No one's hurt,

Nothing has fallen to earth. The arcs of the high
    Bridges are firm. The horses rise
Unbroken from fountain pools, their nostrils flaring,
    Their flanks streaming with ribbons of light.

The drums are muffled. The rain decamps. The sky
    Clears of its clouds, the all-clear siren
Begins to lift its buoyant high C
    Over the dripping gardens of the city,

Luxe, calmé, et volupté, a breath-
    Taking note, like Bix Beiderbecke
Before his face and his talent were ruined by gin,
    When his "tone sounded like a girl saying yes."

MEMORIES OF TEXAS FALLS

Reader, if "dark matter" is hardly the latest mystery
    By the time this pulse has caught your eye,

For us it remained the end of knowing, an unplumbed source
    Where all our figured tales reverse

Themselves and vanish. No blue dome pierced with stars
    Over the steaming baths of the harem,

No row of white columns high on the cliff, framing
    Panels of air where re-told tales

Unfold themselves. . . . in the middle distance, one more time,
    Each scene is printed in the mind

Indelibly, even ours today, in the plunging gloom
    Of Texas Falls. All afternoon

We have heard the echoing drops of a slow, receding rain
    In the far corners of its deep space,

We have seen the ferns and oaks clustered on ledges, and pines
    Climbing the steep slopes to rise

Out of sight, erased in cloud. Is this depressing?
    A vacuous landscape represented

As if a beholder existed? It would be, except for us.
    Seen from above, we are its genius,

Our red and blue umbrellas like blooms of instant feeling
    In a signature scene of Hiroshige's:

Two travelers crossing a bridge, leaning at the rail,
   Bending our heads together. The falls

Disappear downstream in zigzags of fractured rock.
   Mist, below us, rises like smoke.

We were here a decade ago, returning, as you insisted,
   To unriddle our story, an exorcism

Of that day—as if the world were ours to make or dismantle
   At will—we raged like Titans in a tantrum,

Hurling our words back and forth like rocks and uprooted
   Trees, for what? Our source (in Rubens'

Device, a brooch inscribed with a cameo scene from Ovid
   Dangles on the breast of a panting lover

To implant a scene in the scene, cautioning against Unbridled
   Love) our source was my "manic flight"

Years before to the same site (I *could* name names
   But *Why not say what happened* is dangerous

Advice) with the spritely X who later would cry Roberto!
   Every five minutes or so

In looping late night calls, as if she was suddenly startled
   By recognition—we imitate art

Or its lunacy, each revision of the blank box a version
   Of a possible world, virtual and eternal,

But if the cosmos is *not* infinite, instead collapsing
   In a "cataclysmic crunch"?—or is that

Yesterday's question—even if Hubble's "powerful lenses
   Can probe the distant past," by then

It may be too late. When one has counted nine and fifty
       Swans at Coole, and more, it isn't

Easy to recall what happened, let alone reproduce
       The faint flush of seducer or seduced,

But the longing to know persists, as if our last temptation
       Were to track a saga's receding shape

Back to its source, in particles ever smaller, scenes
       Disclosed within scenes until we see,

Again, the same bridge, where a poet who won the year's laurels
       (In a black and white snapshot of the Falls)

The favorite of gods dethroned, and by the time you read this,
       Forgotten, gazed down at a lissome

Girl who was smiling up. Betrayal. Is this the center
       Of the matter, and all the oracle meant

To tell us? There must be more. Another year, she became
       The brown-eyed Carol, our deeply-gazing

Pre-Raphaelite whose low, liquid voice essayed
       "Insupportable hypotheses,"

A spark along a forking branch, last sighted south
       Of Miami with a speedboat-racing crowd,

And gone, where "circumference grazes the void," lost from view
       Out where sightlines are all askew

And our stories dissolve. But if our center *is* a speck
       Clinging somewhere to the outer edge

Of a disk, or is it bubble, beyond—is this depressing?—
       Hubble's "ghostly errors of measurement,"

Our plots are our salvation—and to the friend who complained
    My meandering text was a thinly veiled

Version of the poet's album called *Some Girls,* may I introduce
    Two Gentlemen, dull, sublunary

Mortals, or morons, Mr. X and Mr. Y.—
    Remember them? X's wife

Burned your letters, and who could blame her, blotting all trace
    Of the Other Woman from *his* tale—

An exorcism! But sweetheart, why should we seek to reverse
    Our course, becoming *as we were*

("Before we met"), our stories swallowed up in their origin,
    All forgotten, all forgiven,

If we *live* to tell, by telling our stories (again, lover!),
    One more time, over and over?

"It doesn't matter," Sandage said, "if I feel lonely
    About the cosmos or not," but we

Think it does. The black lacquered box is filled with all
    We feel, and without us, Texas Falls

Has only memories of itself, of endless anonymous pines,
    Of oak and fern clustered tightly

On ledges, of plush moss on blocks of granite—fractured,
    Tilted, and polished by pouring water

To a marble smooth as the skin of a dreamy nymph in a pool,
    By Bouguereau—and whose ideal

Artifice is that, but ours, sighted in the Musée D'Orsay
  Somewhere up or down its maze-

Like granite rooms and zigzag iron stairs, and imported here
  As a signature: *We are here.*

We have heard rain dropping from leaf to leaf, and unseen
  Lives stirring in beds of needles

And mushrooms inching on fallen trees. We have seen
  The river turn to mist. We have been

Two travelers crossing a bridge, under pulsing blooms
  Of plum red and teal blue,

Seen from above. They have paused in their long, rainy journey,
  Before continuing on their way

Together—an image at the heart of the matter, or so at times
  They think, indelibly printed in the mind's

Gloom: figures in a landscape, a row of white columns,
  And floating stars inscribed in a dome.

TELL THE TRUTH

To claim, at a dead party, to have spotted a grackle,
When in fact you haven't of late, can do no harm.
Your reputation for saying things of interest
Will not be marred, if you hasten to other topics,
Nor will the delicate web of human trust
Be ruptured by that airy fabrication.
                          —Richard Wilbur, "Lying"

You wake and reach for the phone. No one is harmed
If you call your wife to claim you have seen the Pacific
At dawn, running for miles over the quick
Blossom-and-fade of an image, on the glassy sand,
When the mist and the lightly stippled sea were a single
Tone of gray. A simple invention. Meanwhile,
Far below, the trackless beach and the green,
Heaving ocean are beginning, only now,
To be disclosed in the wide panes of your room.
You wake alone. What have you done? Nothing,
Or next to nothing, or let us say, you have altered
The sense of a thing in its telling, like Conrad's Nostromo,
The fallen hero who stole the silver he was trusted
To guard. He wakes alone, on the half-moon beach,
On the island where he hides the cargo of ingots. To account
For this loss, he begins to invent a vita nuova,
For his life is his to shape, a lump of wax,
A blank, a dead space to fill, like the ceiling
Of your neutral room, which you now begin to fill,
Lying in bed, first with a fervid blue
From Annibale Carracci, and then with white and gray
Bursts of billowing cloud, edged in pink.
Up the vaulting space, muscular figures
Stream, with red robes aswirl, with arms
Outflung. Their eyes are wide, their mouths agape,
They are all ecstatic, or alarmed, or they are racing

To bring the news of what they have seen, faithful
To fact, but greatly heightened. They are disarming
Messengers, and their words have designs on us—
"I saw the figure five in gold," or "I caught
This morning morning's minion." It does you no harm
To believe them, although you long to be as simple
And passionate as the dawn, the unequivocal angel
Who glides down a single gilt diagonal
To the truth, speaking without premeditation,
Stirred by nothing but the factual world as given,
A colorless wind that spins the aluminum turbine
Blades to a silvery blur, and shakes the wind-chime's
Bamboo tubes into random, artless song,
A few notes, in the quiet evening, on the porch
Where we sit together and say, we have had enough
Of projecting ourselves into dramatic scenes,
Insisting on a rapturous witness of the world, in words
That crackle and flash, in which the snowy egret,
Arriving early in the marsh, is the white dove
Of heaven. But then, who knows what messengers
Cloak themselves in flashy forms, to streak
Across the blank screen of our days, with news
We need but have failed in our humble insistence on fact
To imagine? Say that the fall of the Angel of Light
Is neither defeat nor confession, but a brilliant device
Sustained in space, deceiving the eye, a banner
Unfurled, of radiant particles, a billion times
Told lovelier in our retelling. The world
Is not betrayed if we fall in love with the colors
Of distant horns, echoing in the valley of their saying—
"Go tell the Lacedemonians, that here
Obedient to their orders we lie"—sheerest words,
Faithful to the case of a world only in part
Our own invention, designed to alter or heighten
All that befalls us in our long fall.

ANGELS

To be single-minded
Was the aim of the regimen those winter mornings,
Pure mind in a chastened body, circling
    The lake, to see the arms

Of the pines pressed
Down in severest black and white. . . .
A world reduced to form, in brilliant rooms
    With shimmering bands

Of red and green,
Or willowy, watery sweeps of blue
And purple, is an easy text, with its over-
    Simplified signs like a rainbow

Spray veiled
In olive-drab to complicate mystery,
But out here, plodding counter-clockwise
    Around the water, to see

The world as figure,
Pattern in the pattern, is to see with a stripped
Clarity who in his right mind would seek? To lift
    Layer after layer from a sleeping

Beauty, filmy
Disclosures, like Fragonard's angel, until
The pulsing secret is naked, laid bare,
    Was that the point? You saw

White vapor
Lifting in skeins from the sheer skin
Of gray half-frozen ice pressed to the lake
    Like a billiard table's taut

Green felt
On slabs of slate, cloven, quarried,
Their clay and shale secrets locked in the dense
Grain, secure, unreadable

As random notions
Capped by the polished black marble
Sheet of Truffaut's grave, down a leaf-choked
Alley in the Cimetiére Montmartre.

Think of the vision
Of Sacramento as the plane descended
From 30,000 feet, toward the bay at midnight,
A gold-pulsing screen

Of light in dense
Grids of glowing overlays compacted,
Pattern on pattern. Who was the mystery guest
Who leaned across your seat

To say, you
Will never understand the book you are reading,
Or the news, if it ever arrives, from the Hubble telescope's
Million polished eyes?

FALSE DAWN

Wellfleet Harbor

Awake before waking, to what, a slow brimming
Of toneless light, a flurry of thirty-second notes
Descending, gone . . . a cat bird? Almost dawn.

You try not to stir. A blanched word
Floats in a distance resembling, you think, Claude's
Horizon, blue diminished to blue no longer

A color but a longed-for escape or return, where the sea
Turning inland is a winding stream wrapped
To the bank, where you are the pensive figure saying

False dawn. Whether to elude or embrace,
Hopelessly, the mind chimes in response, *false-
Vaulted casemate,* which is, what, the name

For a sleight-of-hand to feign an arch, a word
You found near Mycenae one bright morning.
How lucid and intact it is: the Aegean spangles

Gold-on-green. At Tyrins the tan, beveled
Stones unfold their ruled crenellations, stately,
Across the hills, a shapely text unveiling

Secrets. How one loves the impassioned drudgery
Of names, decoding a bunker, a mosque enjambed
With Venetian stone, the world demystified.

It's already hot this morning on the roof garden
Of the Hotel Paradise. The waiters remember Farouk
And his babbling retinue, their tubs of oysters,

Their hundred-dollar tips. Tutored Spartans
Thrum on waves plated with Nestor's gold.
Within the passage at Tyrins, its hollow walls

Roofed with an elegant solution, the false-vaulted
Casemate, you see, framed in a narrow embrasure,
The "political prison" rise like a dream. Its white

Walls flake and blaze. Shadow-figures
Climb in the tall, barred half-moon windows
Keening their eerie, unintelligible songs.

Hopelessly, I think of a morning when ice-gray
Half-light spread across the snow and floated
Thinly like a hovering tone through a bubble window

Set in the angled "cathedral ceiling" down
To an improvised bed, our rapt mindless gestures
Thrown together, dissolved, gone. Sunlight

Blazoned the house, dispelling, what, those pale
Legs, a flash of orange hair (your ludicrous secret),
A sudden flurry of small quick cries

Rising in the high room. In a blank incandescence
The too-rapid notes of unidentified song
Drop away. We sleep in our outward selves,

We dream of waking again. . . . Each morning
When the gray-blue horizon is webbed with the wide
Vaporous sea, a globed question rises

To the place where you wait, listening on the edge of waking.
You try to avoid proposing an answer, an actor
Easing across the stage in dream-like evasions

As slowly as he knows how to move, who lifts
His words in pantomime, passing along
The swift, sheer, opaque elisions of air.

CONVERSATION WITH A DEALER, ABOUT A PAINTING IN PRIVATE HANDS

"One wearies of looking for all that's *not there*
        In Monet, in the brainless shimmer, the whirl
Of his vast ambition, to be absorbed in the airy
        Flora of the other world,"

Or so my general theory goes, your answer
        To which is "listen we're talking five million
Bucks of painting here." Or at least we were.
        The sale, yesterday's thrill,

Is off. Today you're looking for "anything French
        Of a certain size," needed by a Japanese
Client for a corporate gift. You shrug. "My business
        Is mainly crap . . . but these

I keep for myself," opening a drawer of prints
        With a showy gesture, a cooperative hush,
As the trilling phone and the chatter of the FAX machine
        Pause—a lion cub

Curled up for a snooze. . . . Delacroix! You roll
        The vowels of the over-valued and -wrought
Name, transporting us to the great hall
        Where heroes translate thought

Into action or cash. In another drawer, an image
        Of the minimal world emerges, its lines
Of black laconic, positing faith in the limitless
        Power of space: an implied

Canal, a bridge, and two figures in reverie,
        Simple men, we like to assume,
Obedient to the blunt instructions of their master: be
        Composed. Tell the truth.

Pissaro: we revere the man, we say, for the anarchist
        Views of your youth, or his pure refusals
Of other-worldly glitter, contradicting
        Ourselves to save our souls.

"MOB RULES"

"Has it ever occurred to you
That the people who write
On walls are organized?"
                    —Mary B. Campbell

Our text, class, is chaos. We are its authors. These words,
Our illustration, are random and senseless, until the rules
To reveal their sense are revealed, or invented, like the laws of cells,
Or quarks, or "dark matter:" a red graffito, MOB
RULES, sighted in darkest Brighton, Mass., where Chaos
Wears the mask of a city, rational once but now anarchist-

Ically sliced and diced by turnpike and "urban renewal." An anarchist
Circle A sprayed nearby suggests the words
Are protest's blunt instrument, or a dadaist text: "Chaos
Is the shark who rolls and rockets bluely beneath the rules
Of Western Civ.," disclosing *l'homme politique* as a mob
And "social science" as nonsense, random as the rioting cells

Of lymphoma. Terror Reigns is the text in the study-cells
Of the local commune. Or the words are an anti-anarchist
Warning, sternly parental, "where there are no rules, the mob
Is the only ruler," or the words advise, "the mob's word
Is law down here. Obey it or die. Patriarcha rules."
If our readings reel and roil, this is the nature of chaos,

According to physics' *enfant terrible.* His theory, called CHAOS,
Says turbulence rules. To prove this point, his convection cell
Models shadows of rolling air, unmasking rules
Of nature's inherent disorder. "Disorder," the Spanish anarchists
Argue, is the heart of a natural order. When Foucault's words
Enlarge their text, a sprawling theory reveals "the mob"

18

As "socially constructed." Meaningless words. Wasn't the mob's
Face plain in the New Mexico prison riot? Chaos!
"To survive, you acted crazy and waved a knife"—no words
Could help the informers trapped, decapitated in their cells.
Random? In the Civil War Draft Riots, the "anarchists"
Were Irish, their victims Black. Class, there are *always* rules.

I unearthed these for our found-poem, MOB RULES:
"Mission of Burma" was a punk-rock band (they ruled!) and MOB
Their acronym. In their thrashing concerts, an anarchist-
Ic rampart of snarls, disorder was the order of the day, and chaos
Was play. After slam-dancing and stage-diving, their cells
Of unemployed zealots wandered out to spray these words

On walls. Thus our précis: "CHAOS" unfolds the rules
Of anarchist nature, and structuralism the law of the mob,
While poets, plotting in their cells, deface the world with words.

VENICE OBSCURED

Paris, July 1989

In the narrow shade of the rue du Temple's
Cous-cous and curio shops, to discover
These pictures everyone's seen too often
(A slender, wincing Vietnamese "traitor"
At the instant of death and Lee Harvey Oswald's

Grimace and recoil from the briefly infamous
Jack Ruby) confirms exactly
What Baudelaire feared. The new "startling
And cruel" medium would not be art
But reproduction, brutish and ubiquitous.

How could a photograph compete with the deep
Glow and shimmer of an image in the mind,
Like the slow evaporation of light
At Giverny? The notion was grotesque.
They rested their case (who could foresee

Steichen, Stieglitz, celestial nudes
Of Edward Weston, the all-new
History of Art unspooling from Daguerre's
First studio—a block from here—
I pass it going for the *Trib*) when Proust

Summed up, "the very word Venice
Arouses more sensations in the mind
Than the most artful photograph"—even if
They arise from *The Wings of the Dove*
And Canaletto. We see, from above,

The piazza where a deep, angling shadow
Offsets a dubious gold and cloaks

The colonnade in narrative gloom.
Vows forsworn, liaisons contracted,
A breath caught at the sudden clasp

Of a hand, entanglements spun from the two
Matte vowels and a *v* and soft
C of VENICE, city in the news
This morning, a water-borne rock
Concert having left the canals clogged

With debris (which is where the art-versus-
Technology issue has washed us
Up, "sensations in the mind" crowded
Out by instant networks of junk-
Bond imagery spent in a blink).

According to the *Herald Tribune* (which I can't
Read without thinking of *Breathless*
And Jean Seberg hounded to death
By the CIA), no one in Venice foresaw
The rabble's Woodstockian aftermath,

Doorway and courtyard fouled with shit,
A government rocked by a muddy, reverberant
Wash of chords, although (the *Trib*
Continues) not everyone was a barbarian
If the audience included Woody Allen

And Mia Farrow (who was? . . . an old
Flame of Frank Sinatra, who
Procured for Kennedy and Sam Giancana
The beautiful Judith Exner and so
On), Sting, Madonna, Arsenio

Hall, a paparazzo's paradise—
Judy, Vanna, whoever, in a flash,
Vaporized, the fifteen-minute

Lives pile up. We swoon over trash.
In the great municipal hall of Venice

Officials rise, asking forgiveness
For "errors in judgment" but the opposition
Sees its chance and refuses to let
Them speak. "Fools!" they cry, "Scoundrels!
You have turned Venice into a toilet!"

OLMSTED'S FENS CORRECTED
BY SHIRCLIFF

Aroused by the way it sounded, *fens*—
Compact, dense, with secrets one could reveal
In a slow disclosure, a kindling, of *glade, glen,*
A flare of darker green, unhearable sounds
Of water fingering through spongy soil—

You brought the word back in your steamer trunk,
A lens: one could see that the raw, prosaic banks
Of Muddy River, if disguised, would emerge
More beguiling, sinuous, mazier than they were
In nature, if cloaked in nature, secrets sunk

Within secrets. When you thrust the river underground,
Insinuated in hidden pipes, your lagoons
Unwound and languished in green, random spaces,
Off-balance and shadowed, like the beckoning recesses
So alluring, in stone, to your neighbor Richardson,

Of the barrel-chest, the vaulted bellow, your swinish
Guest and dark familiar. You lived on coffee.
He dyed the air with dripping joints of beef,
Chewed up blueprints and spilled out designs
For warehouses, trains, jails, wasting the night

While you dozed and schemed, another way to loop
Two woodland paths, a pair of wooded rivers,
Loosely together as if by chance, seduced
To a darker wrestle, in loam, in shadow, lovers
Vanishing to reappear draped in more elusive

Words, altered by their secrets. But soon
You slept for good in sandstone, and your rotund friend

Did too. This is where Arthur Shircliff comes in.
The fens, he concluded, alarmed, were far too unruly.
He sealed the underground pipes. The pools

Where weeds had spun in dark swirls
Like hair in sleep were reduced to a stream
Beneath a wrought-iron footbridge, lacy, petite. . . .
The leftover river he dumped in the Charles.
A new broom. A new expanse, pristine,

Platonic, unrolled from Isabella Gardner's palace,
Clean as a parade ground, a tabula rasa.
Gravel walks radiated out from the core
Of its compass. Tulips braced in the formal
Declamatory gardens. This was no place

For a willful shadow, carelessly flung, a blur
Of green, dark as the red Médoc, black
Where Richardson sits by his torch, where he turns
In his vast chair, and hails you. None of that.
Of what is hidden, veiled, withheld, not a word.

PART II

SUMMER AND WINTER
AT THE MOUNT

1975 and 1985

1.

Lost souls in Chekhov watch the fireflies emerge
From the woods, haltingly, and mope: "One day we'll know
The reason we have lived and why we have worked,
And soon winter will come to cover us with snow"—

In our case, we prayed for summer, for the accomplishment
Of its round tones. When it came, we scavenged the green
World for alternate selves, frantic as aesthetes
From the *fin de siécle* on a querulous tour of the continent.

The Tempest saved us. One midsummer night,
A spritely poly-accented troupe arrived
At Edith Wharton's "Mount": white, Palladian,
But her own design, down to the last brocaded

Bolster, complete, and abandoned when her husband's mind
Shattered. In the shuttered windows, lights
Came on. Below the sloping lawn, released
Spirits poised to spring from the webbed trees.

Now our lives could begin! At the porch railing,
Whole in a flick of hissing light, a young sailor
Leaned to wrestle an invisible wheel. Voices
Blinked from the pines. Present, restored, we rejoiced

To find ourselves marooned in their company, lost,
Where being there together could be enough at last.

2.

Today, ten years later, more or less
The same, we've returned. It's winter in Lenox, Mass.

We circle her flaking house, rehearsing our bleak
Themes (the life or the work, marriage or betrayal).
The brilliant crust breaks beneath our feet.
Distraught calligraphy! Snow lies in draped

Folds on the paired stairways falling like the arms
Of Undine, alas, dropped to her sides in petulant
Exasperation. Poor thing, she's exhausted. Her charmed
Innocence is all in the mind of her husband, the poet

Manqué. What's to be done? A crow veers
Overhead, a scratch of sound across the scene.
No company. What's here but our wish to be here
Completely, to compose the music for a new season,

To weave a new life for Edith Wharton and the slanting
Ghost in the dark hallway, the mad husband?

3.

Let their voices emerge altered in a dimming light
Where sonorous imagined spouses at last grow wise

Together. We pray that their spirits may be beguiled
As they were the summer Edith's guest, arriving
With his great valise of overlaid intonations,
Was the portly Henry James. *Enchanté!*

What more could she have wished—a marriage of minds
In supple talk, all afternoon in her patterned
Gardens, their white petals trembling *en pointe,*
Distinct. Shadows disentangle from the pines

And lengthen over the lawn, which becomes an obedient
Wave rolling to the porch where the lamps are lit,
Where he opens the book he has brought to read, and reads
Aloud, *Leaves of Grass,* its looping anapestic

Flow a counter-spell to their own interiors,
Landings where her confessions are staged, and corridors
Crossed with odd moted lights, suggestions
He greets as *mon bon.* But tonight their labors are set

Aside as he leans to his book and she leans back
In the high-backed brocaded chair, as he croons
The phrases sonorous and strange. Her rings catch
In the lamplight. How hard her mind is tonight! How soon

Winter will come again with work and snow
And trooping hallucinations of death the distinguished
Thing. How clearly he sees it, his work finished,
In the glow of her assembled lamps flowing

To fuse with the dusky pines and the cedars dim,
The tallying chant, our presence conjured, our winter

    4.

Eluded again. It's an August night. From the verge
Of our backyard, the plucked voices emerge

In halting rhythm, like fireflies the dazed, lonely
Ruskin saw in Tuscany, and labored to describe
In a last unfinished work: "How they shone,
Moving through the black leaves like fine-broken starlight!"

DESPERADO

Don't try to pretend you know anything
Out here in the dark where the dunes slump away
Illegibly from the black Atlantic,

Where the path twists back on itself
Like a breathless outlaw covering his tracks.
The landmarks all start to look the same,

The crouched, battered pines, the gray brush
Screwed down into the sand. As Hemingway said,
Anyone can be hard-boiled in the daylight—

It's a different story out at land's end
Where humpbacked whales brood in the dark.
Black gusts pour in over Race Point and drift

Inland, over the scoured, flattened hills,
Down in the arroyos, the blind defiles. . . .
Darkness falls like a hammer on the badlands.

Back in our room, a clean-cut lamplight glints
On the bottle of Graves in its silvered bucket.
Our motel, at the marsh edge, is dreamily called

The Moors. Leslie Howard is playing a poet
Sick of language. He wishes he could die.
Bogart is a killer who can't understand him.

He keeps saying, I *wouldn't know, pal,*
Over and over, sounding minimal, savvy,
A genuine tough guy who means what he says.

FIVE VIEWS OF THIS
AND THE OTHER WORLD

1. Matisse Plays His Violin

In the room whose flatness passes for riches
The Unknown Powers are not permitted
To float in the window, as if it were a mirror,
This window I move from left to right
As the light shifts, accumulating patterns
Of Adrianople red. The goldfish shines
In its glass bowl. I stand beside
The window, naked, in blue shadow,
And practice. Nothing is decomposed.
The violin does not burst
Into flame or become a horse and float
Dreamlike over the orange chimneys.

2. Monet Retreats

From peasants I expected still more disregard,
But they saw my project as a call to arms.
If I rowed to the river island to paint,

They cut my boat from its mooring—they pulled
The grain stacks down with their long forks—
They sold the line of poplars for timber.

So I closed the gate on willow and pond.
Each day I gazed on the other world. . . .
The prints of my boots on the muddy bank

Released their deep patterns each night
To the dew. I accepted the world's regard,
At a certain distance, a certain price.

3. Manet Thinks

Glitter is trash. Monet has decided to praise
My seascape but not the figures who appear to relax
On the sand, who turn in unbidden reverie, distracted
By half-conscious mind . . . tall basalt caves
And heavenly billowing clouds . . . their unwilled pasts
Returning, in a figure's shade, an averted gaze.

4. The Ghost of Alfred Sisley Along the Canal St-Martin

I begin my nightly patrol at the hour
The canal gives up its final colors

(The patches of oily yellow and burnt-out orange,
The snaky streaks of copper, the orchid-

Purples nearly black) for a black marble
Slab, polished, so plainly impenetrable

I am not troubled by the old obsession
To see what floated in the blessed zone

Of surface, in the sheerest imaginable layer,
A bluish haze of snow-shot air

Drifting over the mottled wall
Or a glass-blue sheeting of flood water

Like a new layer of sense on the river
I painted yesterday, and the day before.

5. Klee Reports on the Delauneys

Every morning, Klee said,
When Sonia and Robert get out of bed,
They argue about light—how it decomposes
Around the surface of an electric globe.

PHOTOGRAPH

Few birds came to the salt marsh pool's
Blank, clouded surface, plinked with insects
And air bubbles risen from the soft bottom mud.
It widened with the tide each afternoon,

Inching in faint clicks through the standing grasses.
One morning, at low tide, there were two white herons.
I circled the pool. Clustered mussels.
Underfoot, small snails, dense in matted grass.

Horseshoe crab shells like Stone Age helmets,
Battered black curves, mud-clotted, stranded.
The herons slid out on the water. Across the pool
You sat on the porch, a heavy, dark-blue book

In your lap . . . was it the history of labor law?
All those bristling, bloodied decisions, rounding
The century in righteous battle—how much
Was accomplished that is now undone, all unraveled.

Nearly hidden in the bending grasses,
The inlet stream glittered with the tide.
My camera whirred, a dense inner life, intensely tooled.
Pale yellow fingernail crabs skittered away

And the herons looped off, low in the sky,
Following the curved, tufted banks of Dummer's Cove
Toward Wellfleet Harbor. How we long for closure,
The stiff, clear outline of a family portrait,

A life in brief. For example, Hamilton Spence,
The plain-thinking man who dredged this pool
To harvest his crop of rich salt hay,
A ship's chandler. When whalers dropped anchor

He rushed out to meet them. Women looked on
From behind the twisted wrought-iron railings
Of their widow's walks. It was the industry's heyday.
How can one explain a failure to accomplish

So much that was planned, year after year?
Across the stirred pool, I have a picture of you
As you were, that morning, in a blue flowered robe,
Your head bent one way, the herons gone another.

ATTENDING

You try to attend. The white peaks drift
To the window, the Valium, clear in its transparent tube,
Slides along the O.R.'s murmurous, soothed
Air and down to your vein. You hear him say "listen,
They all look like that, o.k.?" The lazing tones

Of his voice, courtly, slide beneath the patter
Of interns. Faces float up in the smoked glass
Window. You listen to the slowed pulse move
In your wrist, to a clicking of knives as the nurse unwraps
And lays them out. He turns to the students and waves

(They love him so!)—"the hard part here is protecting
The nerve"—how easy his drawled words make
This sound, how difficult, to still be fresh
Day after day, a thousand solos obsessed
With sameness and the slightest variation, how strange

The enterprise is: the *tendon achilles* restored
As if it were a matter of the greatest importance.
The students regard a leg rendered in a splash
Of orange Betadyne. He wields his knife with a flourish,
Opening the calf to the heel (a black-rose gash),

And tells you what he sees: "think of a clothesline
Pulled apart, a mess of strands, a frayed
Mop," which now he tugs together and binds
Hard, his arms straining, with a loop of bright
Blue plastic. But you are thinking of Manet's

Dead toreador stretched flat on the packed
Dust of the arena floor, elegant still in black
Tights, the calves bound in white silk hose,
A distant body, numb from the waist. . . . The loose
Mind drifts as he mutters, conducting his gross

35

Clinic for a scant, scattered audience, believing
They attend his every word. Helen, British,
But here a local genius of anesthesia,
Murmurs at your ear, remarking the brushed
Snow-powdered peaks of Camel's Hump. Her clipped

Tones, burred and dry, slip lightly
Over his low southern vowels. You drift
In the skim and flow of their voices, absorbed, idling
Back and forth, and answer yourself, listen,
O.K., for perspective the toreador is right

But the savage contrasts of your leg, its flare
And flash, come out of Goya's *Third of May*.
Smoke blooms from the crowding rifles. What terror
We feel in his white shirt, his arms hysterically
Flung up, and what delight—not history

But paint, over and over. . . . Hissing light
From the box-lantern floods the ground. How much
Manet must have learned from that, how tiring
The ordeal is, to be fresh, to approach as an acolyte
The ordinary day, walking to work (Valéry mutters,

"Degas is a man who brings to the simplest art
Every possible difficulty") and home, as Time
Passes, the surgeon retires to his quiet private
Practice, and Helen goes home to York, the farm
Where the furrowed earth is ribbed with *grisaille* light

At ten in the evening, and later, at midnight, a tractor
Roars up and down, obsessive still in the black
Fields, the high-mounted headlights swerving
Into the dark at the end of each row, back
And forth, at work, compulsive. As you hear the surgeon

Murmur, sewing up, "that's all for today,"
You think of the Darwin a poet heard, "the precise
Beautiful, solid case, from endless observation,
Heroic, until a relaxed, forgetful phrase
Reveals the real strangeness of his enterprise"

And Turner's fanatic rainbow through the mist
Of Lake Buttermere, a single image that would drive
Him forward fifty years, in love with discipline
And dissolution. They unhook the I.V.'s
And wheel you down the hall. The mind drifts

Up the trail to Camel's Hump on a late
October day under the vaulting sublime
Of sky, to the limestone cliff-face (cubes of gray
Splashed with white), to the tall lilies, orange
And yellow, and blue cornflowers at the far side

Of the beavers' pond. If you kneel at the reedy fringe
And look down, through the smoked, glassy
Surface, you can see the whittled branches crossed
And nestled, the slick bark green with mossy
Algae. Bent to the task, you imagine listening

To the flicker of quick, transparent minnows,
Back and forth like a tingling of brushes skimming
A cymbal, and the dragonfly's paired wings,
A pulsing blur, brushing a reflected image.
You attend as if these words and this single

Task were a matter of the greatest moment, above
All else, and you returned, each year, each day,
To the same demand, its slightest variation, renewed,
Elated, obsessed by what is the same and elusive,
Greeting perfect strangers like someone in love.

MARTINIS, MAIDENS,
MIDNIGHT HOURS

John Huston: "I have been obliged to abandon
The ideal life, *martinis, maidens, and the midnight
Hours,* for a lung machine." As long as this angel
Breathes, I'm alive. A poor exchange, for maidens
Whose forms were heaven-sent, for a potent martini's
Cloud of smoke calling the gods to descend,

As they do—in Fragonard's sweetly indecent
La Chemise Enlevée, how attentive the angel
Is, hovering to lift the gown from a maiden's
Dreamy form—though when they will, they abandon
Us, power by power. Day by day, the midnight
Oases of singing maidens and stirred martinis

Recede. Stevens: "Even a *single* martini
Would be a disaster, but we might condescend
To try their lemonade." I have abandoned
All hope of stronger proof that angels
Will come to the door at my lightest knock. By midnight
I'm asleep, watched over by institutional maidens,

The Sisters who represent a standard made-in-
Heaven policy: sign here and abandon
All loopholes (the heaven revolved of martinis
And maidens) to be safely within the fold when midnight
Strikes, clanging its doors for your descent.
I still recall (though now I answer only the Angelus)

How in the *Departure from Cythera* Watteau's angels
Boil like a cloud of vapor—rising or descending?—
Above the waiting boat. Ladies who were maidens
When they arrived, having so completely abandoned

Themselves, glow supernally, like Simone Martini's
Lost portrait of Petrarch's Laura, like a midnight

Sun . . . but enough (surely?) from these old midnight
Ramblers with their passé views (how "maiden"
Smells of its courtly, detumescing descent!),
Wise guys who thought they'd covered the angles
(Like Sherwood Anderson who swallowed the olive in his martini,
And the toothpick), these stoics, God-abandoned,

Who believe the angels will sing if they abandon
Midnight gloom for calm, while the god descends
As a maiden, *La Source,* pouring a pitcher of martinis.

ONE MORE TIME

Chicago, 1954

But what would it be? The exact word
For a premonition of hopeless loss, as the empty sky
Turned pale green, or the catch in her voice
At the first hesitation, like a pause

In the young Sarah Vaughan's phrasing, or less
Than a pause, as if pure nuance were possible.
After a while, it isn't any clearer.
The Lucky Strike, the Chevrolet,

Those precious, period details, only name
What we're always longing to describe,
The indecipherable gloom
In Turner's emptied drawing room, swarming outward,

Or Constable's sky, constantly more clouded.
A gray wash brushed on a darker gray expanse
Is a cloud on the sea, described, or recalled.
Now, wind sweeps mist across the packed sand.

There are the wavering margins of the salt meadows
Where we walked twice, once in anger
And once hand in hand, naming the grasses.
Black grass is a darker green.

How are we to speak
Of precisely this, in an endless shifting
Away from one moment, toward another, just as it was?
In the Blue Note Lounge one August night

Joe Williams that sweet young man had his eyes closed
As he turned his head from side to side
Singing *Come back baby!*
Let's talk it over, one more time.

OUT OF THE BLUE

There is another shore, another world,
Somewhere, compared to which our own
Pales. This was the dreamy notion
Raised around you like a translucent dome,

The pure transcendent in off-white marble,
Absorbing reflection. It explains your dutiful reading
Of Rilke's *Elegies,* all morning, while heat
From the furrowed sand ripples upward invisibly.

Red and yellow frisbees hover in the air.
Teen-aged Rangers in broad-brimmed hats
Patrol the beach, and a sleek boy, like the muscular
Marriage of a neck and a nun, prances

Beneath his long-tailed kite. Anything is possible,
Even the thought that the fringe of blue
Surf where they wade and kiss is the outer edge
Of the real, the shallows where filmy Medusas,

Half-transparent, rock and float. The sun
Reddens. The air is bluer. Cowboys arrive
In their trucks, unlimbering rod and tackle.
When they cast out, their fine black lines

Repeat a looping illegible scroll
Over and over, like verses on the blue
Walls of the Alhambra. A prowling snorkler
Rises from the surface, like a dream, her wetsuit

Glistening. Someone has heard your call!
She pulls off her glass mask and sprays
Light from her shaken hair. You see? She
Is an angel and all that is the case.

WITTGENSTEIN EATS

The proposition bemused his hostess, and sounded true
Although it was not: "I don't care what I eat
As long as it is always the same thing." The meal
In question was Swiss cheese and brown bread, perfect

For a man who would rather whistle a Bach concerto
From start to finish than play soccer or have sex.
The whistling was thin, literal, persistent, in what
Was otherwise silence, in a long northern winter,

Alone in the room, no one to know if he stops
And turns to another task, or completes the passage,
As he does, and begins it again. This is the music
He wants to hear, the proposition which always

Completes itself, and can be repeated, every day,
The abstract meal, the ideal conversation, a single task
Pressed until it matters more than anything and no
Attention, no repetition, is found excessive.

How could he fail to be disappointed in the world?
Thus the infantile outbursts, storming from the lecture,
Thus the rancor, the rancid taunts, dismissed
From his post for striking a student. . . . How important it was

For the room to be bare: no couch, no rugs, a few
Folded canvas chairs set out when the seminar arrived.
But how tedious, their avid efforts to keep up!
How clear it was in the stark hut with its one

Straight chair, and on the rough table, a knife,
A loaf. An abstract conversation, in silence,
The silence of a life still to be lived, in the absence
Of hope, or the pause between concertos, or the blank

Hours between two meals, to be filled with work
On the next problem. At Cambridge in the evenings
He went to the movies, gangster *noirs,* tight-lipped.
"A good mystery," he said, "is worth more than all

Philosophical texts together." Is there no impatience,
No arrogance or refusal to which he will not stoop?
Who can stand the man! Must we have him to dinner,
To our table, generous and varied, to our company

Of voluble men? This ghost at our feast, this turned-down
Glass? A sullen insistence. The drained voice of what,
In decayed words, we might still say, if we could say
What we mean, and say the same thing each time.

SHELBURNE FARMS COACHYARD, SWALLOWS, SCHUBERT

That you long for someone else, for a figure more intense,
Is no reason to deny the pleasure of this dying

Evening's arrangement: landscape, music, and swallows (a happy
Accident) flittering darkly, diving the pearl-gray air.

Let us say, tonight, it is enough, like Savage Landor's
Old philosopher, loving Nature and next to Nature, art,

Let us agree that the throbbing, agitated surface
Of air, this twilight, is all, if at times we insist

On raw drama and brassy emotion, and are never content
With anything less than the whole world, appalled at ambitions

We discover in ourselves, novelists with a plot for every name
And poets seducing every acquaintance, crazed hungers

For control and loss of control. Swallows in triplets
Bank and dart, past the four musicians whose wrists

Are vibrant and tensed, whose fingering is so rapt,
Whose arms sweep in sudden runs and long swoops

Of swallows down through the stable door, in dark stalls
And out again, as if flung in the air from uplifted hands,

An image, you argue, advancing a theme at the cost
Of clarity, a willful blurring of effect and cause,

But where do any of these arrangements begin
Unless in the rawness of our desires, our longing

For events to occur, to be undone, to be repeated?
For half of your life, you composed half a portrait

Of married bliss. Then, "one day," the predictable
Note, carefully placed, "I've met someone else, this

Amazing feeling will not subside," so. Your life's
Pattern is changed forever in a stroke of apparent

Spontaneity, as if unimagined, like a woman
Who appears in the stable door during the allegro,

Arms folded, her long dark hair pulled tightly back,
Brooding on the music which is everything to her,

So wrapped in self she is unaware of rearranging
Swallows in flight. They swerve, brake, pause in air,

The cello rests in its downward rush, like a kiss
Held back before it is held and held again, the violin

Returning now with a sweet surprise, a simple twist,
Olivier's Othello saying again he loved not wisely,

Only too well, a voice rising at just that point
Where we most expect it to fall, the swallows racing higher

Through rising music, what joy more furious than this
Pursuit with all its power to say yes, or deny,

To repeat the arrangement differently, to gain
The world for the pleasure of throwing it all away.

APRIL IN L.A.

If the point is to duck the conversation—
If you have only two days on the coast
When your brother and his wife meet your plane
With the news of their divorce—

Ask if the Dodgers are at home tonight.
Ask who's pitching. Talk about time
And the weather, the heat, the blurred air.
The carousel clatters in the pauses.

Behind his new, gray, mariner's beard
Your brother is smiling, but at what?
Doreen has gained sixty pounds.
It has been a year since they slept together,

She tells you, and if their story
Lacks surprise, why pretend? They have stepped
From a South Seas novel, stranded figures
By the lagoon, beneath a darkening sky. . . .

The Dodgers host the Houston Astros tonight.
Banks of lights rise on fantastic stalks
Out of the hot, surrounding dusk.
Tiers of seats, painted green, yellow, and blue,

Rise and plunge like a crater.
Strange flowers cling to the slopes.
Beyond center field, beyond the palms
Where the orange Pacific burns,

The sun reddens, wedged flat
In layers of purple and black cloud.
In the upper deck above home plate
The crowd is speaking Spanish.

Headlights circle in the parking lots.
Pitching for the Astros, J. R. Richards!
If you find the game, from this high perch,
Lilliputian, absurd, if they find it dull,

Find another topic. They hated
The "explicit sex" and Marlon Brando
In *Last Tango in Paris*. It's art,
You argue, self-scrutiny, but listen,

Is this a serious conversation?
Do you remember, when we were kids,
The t.v. show *This Is Your Life*?
Mystery guests hid behind a curtain.

When they stepped out of your past
And onto the stage, you had to pretend
To be surprised, laughing, weeping,
Shaken by a moment of true feeling.

Light drains from the canyon.
Profuse, precarious, no two the same,
Fifty thousand blossoms cling.
Above the massed lights, the sky

Is black as lava. A white mountain,
Streaming, lifts from an oily sea. . . .
White sheets were hanging on a line,
Drying slowly in a warm basement

Where the furnace window burned orange
Like the half-moon dial of the old radio.
Vin Scully, Voice of the Dodgers,
Talks about the batters and their histories

In loving, patient, endless detail,
A familiar voice, a lacquered surface

With a dark mahogany rise and flow,
A deeply carved, curved rocker

On the cottage porch when the first lights
Tremble in the lake, and clouds of gnats
Part at the wave of a hand.
The man and woman rest their poles

And let the boat drift in.
It bumps against the rubber tires
We have nailed to the dock. Summer
Has just begun. Everyone is here.

HEAVEN ON EARTH

Crumbs, seeds, who knows what they find
    To eat in the unlikely
Richness of dust beneath the benches—
    Small brown birds

At the edge of Copley Square this Indian
    Summer evening, where men
In blue or gray pin-striped suits
    Linger out in the air

Before heading home, briefly joining
    The semi-permanent residents
On the benches, the seated homeless, and these
    Anonymous birds that pluck

And pick among the half-transparent
    Candy-wrappers and cigarette
Butts. The birds have oval-shaped
    Black and dark-brown

Feathers traced in white, and their tense
    Folded tails twitch
As they walk. A man who looks 70
    But may be only 50

tries to light a cigarette for what
    Must seem to him forever
Until a dapper accountant (or lawyer?)
    Leans to strike his match.

Now he can smoke as well as drink—
    Vodka in pineapple juice.
He crosses his thin legs and braces
    Himself upright on the bench,

Leaning forward to curse anonymous
     Bastards and sons of bitches.
The warm breeze is soft to the touch.
       On the other side of the square

Some girls are kicking a soccer ball
     Back and forth in front
Of three deep Romanesque arches
       Slowly filling with shadow.

From Stanford White's Public Library
     A woman steps stiffly
Across the street, her quick head
       Darting, her hand gripping

A small brown book. Would you
     Like to read it, sir?
Do you speak English? Do you know you can live
       In paradise forever.

PART III

SUNDOWN AT SANTA CRUZ

After dark, when the seals play on the under-
Girding of the pier—grand bathers whose pleasure
Is being seen—light from the new boutiques
Filters down through layer after layer of timbers
To model their viol-shaped flanks. Through esthetics

Is hardly his slant, Steve leads me to where
They are, a shaft sunk in the dock (one wonders
Why, but he should know, who dotes on structures
And their meaning, *viz.,* the wharf's change from productive
Fishery to yuppie mall) where we lean and stare

In the pit until those masses of light and shade
Are seals. Lounging on the soaked beams, they breathe
With calliope toots, resounding shudders and bass
Sighs that *sound* like pleasure—who can say
Why one decides to plash back in the sea

And another heaves up, a triumph of agility. . . .
Earlier today we watched the surfers paddle
Over the combers on their brand-name boards, their shoulders
Rounded by sunset—high relief from the brittle
Vermont winter. For years I've visited Steve

Wherever he was, reporting with an eye like de Tocqueville's
Or Sinclair Lewis at the stockyard: Lowell, Mass.,
Was the worst, a "planned city" of dark Satanic
Mills (drained each year, the canals revealed
Round white infant bodies) but Santa

Cruz is a treat, where the surfers catch a wave
And clamber up, to hold their balance briefly,
Veering from side to side—to make the feat

More difficult? What pure pleasure, pure play,
No more productive than Chartres' vaulting ceiling

Rethought as *higher* each time it burned, a candle-
Eluding darkness raised to awe. . . . As the orange
Sun goes down, some boys are already back
In the parking lots. Perched on the bumpers of four-
Wheel-drive confections, they strip off their black

Wetsuits. The diehards keep it up. I'm thrilled
By their stunts, but Steve grumbles like a jaded railbird
At Hialeah, "this is amateur surf—
The pros know enough to quit." Surely we all
Persist at our fond obsessive tasks, more compelling

Than useful or pleasing? I'm thinking now, unkindly,
Of Steve's laborious novel, unfinished off
And on for how many years—a history of Chinese
Migrants packed in a train steaming cross-
Country to scab a shoemaker's strike is at least

As worthy as, well: if we stopped, would the world be a better
Place? Mary, of her essays on "Gender in Zola"
(Publish or perish), confessed "I'd rather laze
All day like a doll in Ingres, and at night compose
A perfect lyric, like Sappho's . . ." or the *Concert Champêtre*

Where perfectly balanced masses of light and shadow
Are leaf, curl, plush, flesh, a distant
Birdcry, hiss of drapery shrugged from shoulder
To hip, ah, her illumined back where our kiss
Is planted, the dolorous plink of water on stone. . . .

Giving pleasure is never beneath us, as the programmed
Zola knew—think of that dazzling scene
In *Germinal* where the anarchist sets his explosives

In the mine (I've tried for years to get Steve to read
It, grist for his mill). On a turning rope, he lowers

Himself timber by timber down the deserted
Shaft, shadows swimming from the lantern as he plants
The dynamite tubes and wires. His acrobatic
Feat is beautifully seen, and his charmless concerted
Vision, of a new dawn and its old demands.

CHARLOTTE CORDAY'S SKULL

Professor Y's famous concluding speech
Fades in memory like a star redshifting ("Class,
We have learned that we know nothing!"). But you *were* pleased,
Then, by this general theory of your own distraction.
What were you thinking? When a certain slant of sun
From the high library windows blazed in motes
Of spinning dust, and in the hair of the sumptuous
Student of Mao. . . . After years of Hubble's "ghostly
Errors of measurement, out at the dim limits
Of our telescopes," we arrive at these receding
Scenes with the same ardent question, *what is it?*
Have we understood *anything?* The phrenologist believes
His calipers seize the warp of an anarchist will.
His gaze is fixed on her lacquered, lamplit skull.

NEWS

1.

I instantly think of you
When I see it, from a sheer loop
In the highway, far down the plunging
Point Reyes headland by the beaded fringe

Of surf—but the van with fairy-tale flowers
Or whatever it was, a rusting
Carcass now, turned over and crushed
In its long fall, can't be yours—

You died south of here, at Big Sur.
Still, the burnt-umber, caked
Wheels lifted like a sign above the swaying
Grass might have been there

Seventeen years. On the beach near Sounion
After hours of brandy
And sprawling talk, when a low moon
Pulled from the pines, you stripped and ran

Suddenly into the sea, to reappear
Half-draped in a white towel. I stared.
Ghostly fruit, shadow and glimmer.
Seeing you later in the light of *plein air*

Was a shock, like facing *Olympia* for the first
Time, yellow and red in the pale version
Of paradise one had invented.
Now I can hardly remember

All that guilt—can we get in touch?
So much has changed, but we could always fill

Lacunae of our story with new or familiar
Twists on the old theme, *Poets and Lovers,*

At our reunions, years apart, resuming
An abandoned conversation, a plot
Whose roles were assigned and rehearsed—but
Stephanie, tell me, is this really you?

2.

The night we returned from friends lost
Sight of now (Caroline, whose late-
Breaking news of an earlier life, her shameless

Rolls on studio floors like a Rodin girl,
Had shocked her husband) you sat on my lap
Not thinking one hopes of Daddy, but who knows

While we kissed and kissed
And told, redoing this
Arrangement for each new drink, to resume

Our endless loop, kisses and tales
Of poets who sounded in your praise
Like fantasy friends,

Your black sweater unbuttoned,
Warm flesh rosy in the one
Close lamp's glowing pulse. . . .

3.

Am I leaving the right parts out?
Lurid bits that make a story hum,
Parties that came unhinged.
You knew how to rearrange a scene.

The night I had your final news
In a house at Wellfleet

Where ponderous ghosts
Of Nabokov and Wilson grumbled back and forth

Huddled against the fog-horn-
Threaded chill of fall, the toast
I offered fell flat. That recent
Distance between us was then complete,

And changeless until now. "I have found
A job as a topless bottomless dancer"
Your last letter said—were you kidding?
With your sense of rhythm?

But seeing an orchard body
Businessmen seeking love and peace
In a North Beach dive could ignore
The plain face, the bare feet

Slapping the platform out of synch,
And cry with Sappho "I think
You need never bow to any girl, nor one
Who may see the sunlight in time to come."

4.

Whose face did I see in yours
The night you talked for hours,

Stoned? In plots we never see whole,
Are we meant to take bit parts—any role

With new information, new directions
Brought by Iris, Messenger

Of the Gods, as she flies through space
With her leg lifted, her naked

Foot clasped in her hand? Why not,
You said. One night, when the bay fog

Sank on the beaded lights with a sob. . . .
You'd listen to the story and nod,

Who shared tales of your lovers
As narratives to be examined, revered

(How much of your bright irreverent
Mind have I invented?).

5.

Some nights are newly invented,
Some conversations don't recur.
I haven't been called "judge-penitent"
By anyone else, haven't returned
To its source, *La Chute,* for years—

After fifty, one can name
The books one won't reread
(*The Golden Bowl?*) although, who knows.
You died after *V.*
And before *Gravity's Rainbow.*

Pynchon is tremendously
Changed, or so he likes to tell us—
Of the poets you had a crush on, Snodgrass
Is here, if mentioned less,
Lowell is dead, what else—

I published two elegies,
One in *Shenandoah,* the other
In . . . *Stooge?* There!
It's you! I can instantly hear
Your sharp laugh, "not really?"

6.

Really. With a scene meant to shock
(I left the party drunk
And went to bed. Later you clumped
Through the pitch-dark room—"I waited
All evening just to talk
To you!"—and threw back the covers to take me

In hand), suiting the taste
Of hopped-up confessional days.
Are you bored by these seasonal changes,
Or do you follow them, like fashions, one convention
After another, talking to you as if—
The problem is hardly where to begin.

A heavenly day. Wind fingers the yellow
Grass and flicks the blue looping surf
Into white—pure inspiration on a journey
South, from Point Reyes to Big Sur
And the drenched, reddening melodramas
Under the cliffs of Jeffers country,

To join the great promenade, on the boardwalk at Venice
Beach, where dazed, burnt-out souls
Disguise themselves in flowers, fringes
And beads, as if the interludes
In our own plot were now theirs to compose—
I could ramble on and on about this,

Stephanie, I have so much news!

ANTI-MAGIC AT THE PARIS OPERA

The chandelier descends from the blue dome,
On eight woven steel cables, down

To the orchestra floor. Now where banks of glass
And the infinite dimmers hovered above us,

A round hole opens on space, or not
Exactly, but a new world of metal crosswalks

And circling platforms, of levers, gears, and wires.
Staring upward, we instantly fall under

The spell of mechanics. The red plush and gilt
Curves of the best seats have been spirited

Away, and a wide sea of blue plastic
Spread on the floor, where workers circle on hands

And knees, like divers around a wreck. We've seen
All there is to see. No Rite of Spring

And no Damnation of Faust today, only
This reinvention of space, a trompe l'oeil

Thrill: our hectic opus, Redemption and Love,
Unmasked, updated, replayed as particle and wave.

COPYING

1.

Tracing the rim of the pewter bowl, light in Vermeer
has travelled light years

from a source of flame richly imagined
over a space with no shape or end

except for us, posed to receive it,
and the hush of a room where light

on her bare arm and the down of her cheek
is an inner glow, or a layered glaze.

2.

She lifts the brush and adds
a thinned layer,
                        the tip barely touching the canvas
and scrapes the faint smudge of yellow
                           with a cuticle stick—
                                  "Optics"
she says
"is the source"
                of the famous light
constructed it would seem layer by layer
                of cream, pearl, ivory, gold, and rose, but
rising
"really, from the blue underpainting"

heaven help her
as she pokes at the pools of color
on her copper palette, and stalks
        into the corner
        to peer at Vermeer: release your secrets!

3.

Lord send my roots rain is the *prière du jour* for all of us sad sacks and poor passing facts and Sunday painters out so early in the morning pretending to ignore each other in different corners of the far field, also the writer whose second novel in progress for decades was still piled high in typescript when he died, some claim to have seen it, like the famous towers of found objects, towers of trash.

4.

For a moment on the hard wood of the bench
        he feels reduced, like a visiting pilgrim
or a monk
            before sunrise in the cold chapel,
its clumsy but harrowing frescoes hard to see

        the scene emerges
as he thinks about it, as he picks over
materials at hand, Meteora,
a monastery emerging
                from the cliff face
an effect Gaudi could use

to construct the concrete setting
        with layers
of nuance, smudges, scratching out facts
        and adding cloudy pauses
                before and after
            is an exercise
he had praciced long enough
        some nights falling asleep
            with the reed in his mouth
anything to get it right,

                        to manage the light
spreading through the chapel
                thin bluish grey of false dawn

and then pale yellow of winter daylight
stringing the peaks together
                layer after layer
—if having begun with the vaguest yearning he ends
not with the visible form
                of something else but another structure entirely
is it because he lacks an inner life?
        this could explain his penitent air
on a bench at the National Gallery,
                notebook spread on his lap
                        watching a woman copying Vermeer.

    5.

After we saw that Jarrell's girls at library tables and women in
supermarket aisles, toward whom he condescended so easily,
were Randall in drag and self pity at one remove, we protected
ourselves from public exposure by embedding every angle in
the work itself, abstraction hedging its bets with figures and
figures guarded by abstract blocks, so that harried critics, driven
to borrow the wily coyote's paradox, praised our "careful
recklessness," yes! for those who believe you *can* have it all, a
memorable point in our travels, like scholasticism or nouvelle
cuisine.

    6.

Yellow, squeezed from its tube onto the copper palette,
        is a pool of light or a pond
shocked by sunset
                like Saul fallen under the hooves
                        lying on his back with his arms flung up
where the stagy shaft of light comes down

a simple device, crude in its way, but used
        with enough . . . what? brio? courage? it spawns
a century of Caravaggists.

7.

The stroke of genuis, the gesture that moves us, seen once and never forgotten, flows from meditation or passion or sleep or waking in the black of a *noche oscura de alma,* or so they used to say, no one believes that stuff any more but wouldn't the *jeune fille* sell her soul for Divine Sarah's low liquid tone, welling like a pool of tidal light, a swelling legato which years of fretting over angle of wrist and fingers can barely prepare us, should it ever occur, to receive, pilgrims fumbling to find themselves at last in the blessed presence?

8.

She prods
a pool of color and lifts the charged brush toward
        the canvas mounted at a slight angle

this is the moment of truth, a single touch,
        the note struck and the line laid down
                for all the world to see
as Ammons says when the skater
                glides out on ice in front of the hushed crowd

—why commit this folly?

publishing one's first
clipped and bristling verses
                to wide praise
thereafter damned
to reenact in public, in broad daylight, decade after decade,
the closet drama
                of competence,
naked rulers or accomplished scoundrels
        or suave grumblers
                all dressed up with nowhere to go
writing to save our souls
writing as if

only the writing mattered
but when neglected, grown more and more bitter?

9.

Soul we think of as a deep pool aglow with images presumed
to lie within us, as if our potential were infinite, also we think
that our inner being can be betrayed by failing to get in touch
with it, *cf.* "getting in touch with your feelings," once believed
along with Chautauqua lectures and deep knee bends to be a
source of good, as if within our darkness we could somehow
locate a switch for the hissing arclights, and gosh look there's
the Acropolis.

10.

                              Remember you can revise
though not forever
one day it is finished, sold and hung on a wall,
generations die, in pain or not, consoled or not,
prayed for or not, then
                              Berenson buys it for Isabella Gardner
it makes the trip to the USA
and hangs in an upper room at Fenway Court
where Lowell sees it and writes

"Pray for the grace of accuracy
Vermeer gave to the sun's illumination
stealing like the tide across a map
to his girl solid with yearning"

and then the guards are bound and gagged, it is stolen
                and goes back into the dark
        from whence it emerged

now who knows where it is
                kept in a vault as
                        leverage in some murderous deal
or a centerpiece in the diamond-lighted

den of an upper echelon
Japanese mafioso
in Tokyo.

11.

No matter how hard we try, it may still be, gulp, that our work
is "really not good enough, just not very good," what pleasure
we find in saying this, in conversations where someone has to
take it with a grin, in interviews, or wedged into the fabric,
they know who they are, "I wonder what she thinks she's do-
ing," said of a painter who copied others obliviously, by the
laureled novelist taking a break from her lightning raids her
drop-dead rehabilitations of weary genres, her out-of-breath
blowups of new worlds from old junk.

12.

Yes this is it nor are we out of it,
a nostalgic side trip
for the dwindling few who would sell their souls
to tap a source of light
like morning song spreading between two peaks,

one's subtlest feelings
                              having found the right technique
at last, reappearing as pure radiance
falling through the air,
                    the riches we prayed for
if action is prayer,

altering our angle, our distance, day after day,
in the lawns and fields around the aspiring steeple

13.

Naturally, alas, her copy of Vermeer is an abject lesson, *this is
what happens* when inspiration leaves us alone with subject mat-
ter and received technique (Roethke borrowed his cadence,

he said, from Yeats, and Dickey enrolled in his singing school
but "Dickey failed to understand Roethke's meter,"
pronunciamento of So and So who mastered meter but noth-
ing else).

14.

Well if some have taken whole careers to reinvent
a way of stringing sounds together
a brush whirled in the air
pebbles in a hollow stick

longer pauses in the slow rhythm
of two stones knocked together,
                    by the echoing lake,
        the sound floating between two peaks,
music for a flute and drum,

or removing the third actor,
here we are again
or reducing matters further still, a single figure

who moves across the stage, first speaking,
and then without words,
a procession of one, a frieze,
as slowly as the director can make him move,

if the time it takes is the time it takes
who is to say this
                                    is not worth waiting for?

15.

We were kneeling in the vast cathedral but in a corner ignored
by circling tourists, where the sign hung on the metal railing,
Silence et Prière, was strictly observed, on either side of the
homely altar, our awareness of one another sufficient only to know
we were not alone in our delusions, our hopes which rose above
us along with smoke from our candles up to the darkened vault.

16.

Light in Vermeer is divine light
and its source
is what we're after

poor saps,
            duffers and dazzlers and sweetly mournful songsters
of the opaque world,
                        longing for spirit

though what she brings to light, the scales
and what she weighs in the balance, and all that covers
her plump shoulders and her breasts, all that is strewn and hung
around her in the hushed radiance of the room

is Vanitas,
            solid in the hand, assessed
by Stanley rummaging in Blanche's trunk

dredging up the trashy rhinestone and the sequinned tulle
tossing it toward the light

this is a solid gold dress I believe

the white of the fur around her neck
      whiter than white in Vermeer,
      a blue-gold other-worldly irridescence
            but in ours a soap-foam froth

the green velvet thrilling to the touch
the dark-red tapestry worked in gold
the pewter, the silver, the pearl, the coin

drenched in light where our gaze hungers
                              and is fed.

INTERIOR AT PETWORTH

After the mind is emptied
And the empty shell is glowing with light
Paper-thin and translucent

After Goethe's theory of color
After coffee and brandy
And conversation turned like crystal

After Claude's blue unearthly country
And the high plunging sterns
Of the Dutch ships

After the mind
Knows as fact that those
Who have bowed from the drawing room

Will never be back,
When shapeless, dulled shades
Drift in the hollow space:

What has it taken, to come to this,
A secret revealed
One could hardly think hidden?

How light it still is, with no hand
To kiss, no pulse speeded up,
No theory and no source.